Salamander Facts for Kids

Explore the Fascinating World of Salamanders and Learn Everything You Need to Know About Them

Table of Contents

Introduction

Deep in the heart of nature's secret hideaways lives one of the most fascinating creatures to ever exist on this planet. They have been around for millions of years, adapting and surviving even longer than animals who were bigger and stronger than them. Meet the great salamanders. In this book, you will get to learn all about them and explore the hidden corners of their mysterious world. From the tip of their tiny toes to the flick of their long tails, they are absolutely adorable and full of surprises. Did you know that salamanders come in lots of different colors and patterns? Some of the colors are bright and hot, like the sun, while others are cool and calm, like the ground in a forest. Their unique colors make them look like little living rainbows, adding color and beauty to the world. And if that isn't impressive enough, some salamanders can regrow their tails if they lose them. Pretty cool, right?

As you turn the pages, you'll meet salamanders that come in all shapes and sizes. From the tiny pygmy salamander that can fit in the palm of your hand to the majestic giant salamander that can grow longer than an adult's arm, there's so much variety in this incredible species. You'll get to know the secret places they call home. From concealed forest floors to crystal-clear mountain streams, these amazing life forms are masters of camouflage, blending into their surroundings like nature's little magicians.

There's so much more to salamanders than meets the eye, and with this book, you get all the juicy details and fun facts. You'll finally understand the mysteries of how they eat, breathe, and communicate with each other. You'll discover their unique hunting techniques, clever ways of finding food, and even the special dances they perform to communicate with their fellow salamanders. So, grab your magnifying glass, put on your explorer's hat, and prepare for the most exciting mission into the salamander kingdom.

Chapter One: What Are Salamanders?

Salamanders have been around since the time of dinosaurs. Can you believe it? They've been hanging out on Earth for millions of years. Even though the world has changed a lot, these little guys have stayed pretty much the same. They're really good at adapting and surviving in different environments, which is why they're still here today.

Salamanders can be found all over the world. They live in North America, Europe, Asia, and some parts of Central and South America. They're little globe-trotters, making themselves at home in many different habitats. Some love to live in water, while others prefer to hang out on land, but it doesn't matter where they are; they are pretty good at making themselves comfy. From snowy mountains to steamy rainforests, they have a bunch of homes all over the place.

1. Salamanders have been on Earth for millions of years. Source: Bernard Germain de Lacépède, Public domain, via Wikimedia Commons.
https://commons.wikimedia.org/wiki/File:FMIB_37693_Salaman dre_Terrestre.jpeg

Understanding Salamanders: An Introduction

People have always been really, really curious about salamanders, and they have inspired lots of stories and legends. Way back in ancient times, people believed salamanders could survive in fire. It sounds crazy, but that's what they thought. They thought salamanders could even put out flames. This belief made salamanders mysterious and magical creatures in many people's eyes back then.

In medieval times, alchemists (fancy scientists) used the symbol of a salamander in their work. They thought salamanders had special powers that could help them do incredible things, like turning metal into gold. Salamanders were seen as symbols of change and regeneration. The alchemists thought they could learn from them and use their special qualities to conduct amazing experiments. They even drew pictures of salamanders in their books and on their tools to bring good luck to their work. The alchemists also believed that salamanders were connected to fire and could survive its strong heat. This made them even more interesting to study and wonder about. The salamander became a symbol of hope and magic, inspiring the alchemists to keep learning and trying new things, hoping to discover secrets and make incredible changes in the world.

Modern scientists are interested in salamanders, too. They're always studying them and learning new things. You see, salamanders are unique and interesting because they can live in water and on land, so they have special features and behaviors that scientists love to explore. One of the things that makes salamanders really interesting is their ability to regenerate body parts. If a salamander loses a leg or a tail, it can grow it back. This superpower is called regeneration, and it's something that scientists are still trying to fully understand. Imagine if you could grow back body parts like salamanders do. This would change everything, especially in hospitals. Even though humans can't regrow body parts as salamanders do, studying them can help scientists learn how to make it possible for everyone. Scientists are interested in how salamanders can regrow complicated body parts with bones, muscles, and nerves. If they understand how they do it, they might be able to help people who have been hurt or sick and need new body parts. It could be a big breakthrough in medicine. Just think about it: people who have lost their arms or legs could grow them back instead of using fake ones made of plastic or metal. And if someone's heart or liver got damaged, they might be able to grow new ones. It would change their lives completely and make them feel better.

Salamanders are not just interesting to scientists; they are important for the environment, too. They are what people call an "indicator species," which means that their presence or absence can say a lot about the health of the place they inhabit. If salamanders are doing well, it usually means that the environment is healthy. Unfortunately, some species of salamanders aren't doing so well today. Their homes are in danger of disappearing; there is too much pollution, and the climate is changing. This is not good for them or for other animals. That's why scientists and people who care about nature are studying and working hard to protect these special animals. By learning more about salamanders, you, too, can try to make things better for them and for all the other animals living here on Earth. Our job is to take care of them and ensure that they have a safe and happy place to live.

Categories of Salamanders

2.   Cave Salamander. Source: Greg Schechter, CC BY 2.0
<https://creativecommons.org/licenses/by/2.0>, via Wikimedia
Commons.
https://commons.wikimedia.org/wiki/File:Cave_Salamander_(Eu
rycea_lucifuga)01.jpg

Cave Salamanders: Cave salamanders are a type of salamander that lives in dark, wet caves. They are special because they have learned to live underground.

- **Home**: As the name suggests, cave salamanders live in caves. These caves are dark and damp and have cool water in them. They prefer to be in places without light because their eyes are sensitive, and bright light can hurt them.

- **Looks**: Cave salamanders can have different appearances, but they usually have long bodies and smooth skin. They can be brown, gray, or even a pinkish-white color. Some have spots or patterns on their bodies.

- **Breathing:** Cave salamanders have a special way of breathing because they live in dark caves underground. Since caves don't have much fresh air, these salamanders have a clever trick to get the oxygen they need. They breathe through their skin, as many other salamanders do, but their skin is extremely thin, which lets them absorb whatever oxygen they can get from the air in the cave. This helps them survive in places where there isn't a lot of fresh air.

- **Special Skills:** Cave salamanders have abilities that help them survive in dark caves. One of their coolest skills is seeing in the dark. Their eyes are exceedingly sensitive to light, so they can see even when it's dim. They are also great climbers and swimmers. They use their strong legs and tails to crawl over rocks and swim through water. They can even squeeze through small spaces because their bodies are so flexible.

3. Terrestrial Salamander. Source: Chace Holzheuser, CC BY 4.0 <https://creativecommons.org/licenses/by/4.0>, via Wikimedia Commons. https://commons.wikimedia.org/wiki/File:Chiropterotriton_terrestris_2900810.jpg

Terrestrial Salamanders: Terrestrial salamanders that live on land instead of in water.

- **Home**: Terrestrial salamanders live in a variety of places like forests, meadows, and deserts. You can find them hiding under logs, rocks, or leaves. They must stay in damp areas because their skin needs to stay wet.

- **Looks:** Terrestrial salamanders come in different sizes, shapes, and colors. Some are small and slim, like the pygmy salamander, while others can be bigger and chunkier. They all have smooth skin and can be brown, gray, or even bright orange or yellow. They usually have patterns, stripes, or spots on their bodies.

- **Breathing:** Terrestrial salamanders don't have gills like fish. They have lungs, just like all land animals. But they can also sort of breathe oxygen through their skin. That's why they need to be in moist environments to keep their skin wet and healthy.

- **Special Skills:** One of the awesome things about terrestrial salamanders is that they can grow back body parts if they lose them. They can regrow them if they lose their tail or even two legs. This special ability helps them survive and heal if they ever get hurt.

- **Safety:** When it gets very cold in winter, some terrestrial salamanders take a long nap called hibernation. They find a safe place to hide, like under leaves or in burrows, and slow down their bodily functions. This helps them save energy until it gets warmer again.

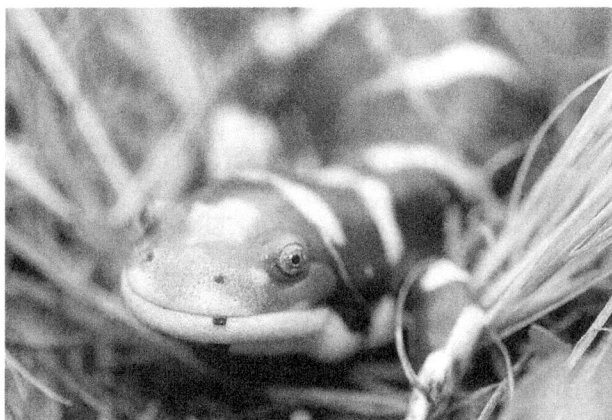

4. *Aquatic Salamander. Source: Heide Couch, Public domain, via Wikimedia Commons.*
https://commons.wikimedia.org/wiki/File:Travis_AFB_works_to _protect_species_120410-F-RU983-066.jpg

Aquatic Salamanders: Aquatic salamanders are special salamanders that live in water.

- **Home:** Aquatic salamanders live in different kinds of water, like ponds, lakes, rivers, and swamps. They prefer to be in clean, fresh water because that's where they find their food and places to hide.

- **Looks:** Aquatic salamanders have sleek bodies and smooth skin, which allow them to move easily in the water. They can be different colors, like black, gray, or even sunshine yellow. Some have unique spots on their bodies that help them blend in with their environment.

- **Breathing**: Aquatic salamanders have special body parts called gills that let them breathe underwater. These gills take oxygen from the water, keeping them alive and able to swim around.

- **Special Skills:** Aquatic salamanders have a sleek body shape that helps them swim through the water quickly. Their long, strong tail pushes them forward like a super paddle. Some salamanders even have webbed feet or toes, like flippers, which help them swim even better. They also wiggle their body from side to side, like a snake, to move through the water.

5. *Mole Salamander. Source: Riley Stanton, CC BY-SA 4.0 <https://creativecommons.org/licenses/by-sa/4.0>, via Wikimedia Commons. https://commons.wikimedia.org/wiki/File:Ambystoma_maculatu m_Stanton_1.jpg*

Mole Salamanders: Mole salamanders got their name because they love the underground, just like moles.

- **Home:** Mole salamanders live in different places, like forests, swamps, and grasslands. They enjoy wet soil and being near water, like ponds or streams.

- **Looks:** Mole salamanders have a unique appearance. They are usually dark in color, like black or dark brown, which helps them hide in the soil. A few have spots or stripes on their bodies. They have smooth skin and a slender shape to move through the dirt easily.

- **Breathing:** Mole salamanders have a special way of breathing. When they are babies and live in the water, they use gills to breathe, just like fish do. But when they grow up and live on land, they use their lungs to breathe air like humans do. They also have special skin that absorbs oxygen from the air around them. So, they can breathe through their lungs and skin to get the oxygen they need to stay alive.

- **Special Skills:** Just like regular moles, mole salamanders are great at digging tunnels in the dirt. Their strong front legs and sharp claws help them burrow deep into the ground. These tunnels keep them safe and help them find food.

- **Safety:** When the environment gets too dry or hot, mole salamanders take a special nap called estivation or brumation. They find a safe spot underground and slow down their body functions until things get better.

Axolotl Salamanders: Axolotls are special salamanders that spend their whole lives in water. They are sometimes called "Mexican walking fish," but they are not really fish.

- **Home:** Axolotls are originally from specific lakes in Mexico called Lake Xochimilco and Lake Chalco. They like to live in calm, fresh water with lots of plants.

- **Looks:** Axolotls have long bodies and adorable faces. They come in different colors, like pink, white, and gray. Unlike other salamanders, axolotls look cute like babies even when they grow up. They never turn into grown-up salamanders as their cousins do.

- **Special Skills:** One amazing thing about axolotls is that they can regrow body parts. If they lose a leg, part of their tail, or even their heart, they can grow it back. Another salamander can do this, remember?

7. Giant Salamander. Source: Momotarou2012, CC BY-SA 3.0 <https://creativecommons.org/licenses/by-sa/3.0>, via Wikimedia Commons.
https://commons.wikimedia.org/wiki/File:Japanese_Giant_Salam ander_(Andrias_japonicus)_Stuffed_Specimen.jpg

Giant Salamanders: Giant salamanders are the biggest salamanders in the whole world. They can grow to be as long as a tall, grown-up person. That's really, really big.

- **Home:** These special salamanders live in rivers, streams, and lakes in places like China and Japan. They like to hide in the water and under rocks during the day and come out at night to look around and find food.

- **Looks:** Giant salamanders might look a little scary to some people because of their size, but they are very calm. They have long bodies, strong legs, and a very big head. Their skin is usually dark-colored, which helps them hide well in their watery surroundings.

- **Special Skills**: Giant salamanders are excellent swimmers. They have a sleek shape and a powerful tail to glide effortlessly through the water. Their strong legs help them move around and catch their favorite snacks. They also live for a really long time compared to other salamanders. If they have a safe environment and plenty of food, a giant salamander can live for many, many years.

So, what have you learned so far? Salamanders are amazing animals that live both on land and in water. They come in all sorts of colors, shapes, and sizes. They have some really cool tricks, like their ability to regrow lost body parts and their different ways of breathing. You've also learned that salamanders are great at hiding, using their colors and patterns to disappear into their environment. In the next chapter, you'll learn about their homes and why they are important to them and to the environment.

Chapter Two: Salamander Habitats

Salamander homes are teeny-tiny worlds full of life and many different animals. Everything is connected in a special way, like a big puzzle. It's a mini-universe just for them. Each part of their home is important and helps keep their world happy and healthy. In these tiny worlds, salamanders have cozy spots where they can hide and rest. They like to hang out under logs and rocks, where it's cool and safe. The ground there is always a little damp, which helps keep their skin moist and healthy.

8. *Salamanders share a home with other animals, too. Source: Christian Votteler, Public domain, via Wikimedia Commons. https://commons.wikimedia.org/wiki/File:D%C3%BCrigen,_1897, _T05.JPG*

But salamander homes aren't just for salamanders. Many other animals live there, too. You might find busy bugs, chirping birds, and playful squirrels in the forests. In the wetlands, colorful dragonflies zip around, frogs make funny sounds, and turtles enjoy the sun. Even underground, worms, spiders, and beetles share the salamander's home. Everyone in the salamander's world has a job to do. Some bugs become tasty snacks for the salamanders, giving them energy. Birds and other animals accidentally help plants grow by spreading seeds around, and the worms dig holes in the ground that allow water and air to reach the roots of plants. It's a big team working together to keep everything in balance.

And guess what? The salamander's home is connected to other places too. The plants make the air fresh; insects help flowers grow, and even the leaves that fall on the ground help new plants grow. By understanding how everything fits together in salamander homes, you can learn important lessons about how you can take care of the world. Just as in their tiny universe, every creature, no matter how small, is important and has a role.

Where Do Salamanders Live?

Salamanders live in many different places all around the world. They can be found in forests, wetlands, mountains, and even in your backyards. They like to live in cool and moist environments because they have delicate skin that needs to stay wet. Here are all the places you are sure to find a salamander:

- **Forest**

Many salamanders love to make the forest their home because it provides everything they need to survive and be happy. You'll find salamanders hiding in some pretty cozy spots in the forest. Look under fallen logs, rocks, and even the layer of leaves covering the ground. These hiding places are their bedrooms, protecting them from hungry predators and extreme weather. As you know, salamanders have very delicate skin that needs to stay wet to stay healthy. Luckily, the forest floor is covered with layers of leaves and soil that keep things nice and wet.

9. Salamanders in the forest have plenty of delicious food to eat. Source: https://www.pexels.com/photo/green-grass-on-forest-418831/

Salamanders in the forest have plenty of delicious food to eat. They love to munch on insects, worms, and even spiders; the forest is basically a giant restaurant serving up all their favorite treats. Everywhere they look, there's something tasty to munch on. This is because everything is connected to everything else. The fallen leaves on the ground create a cozy home for the salamanders, and when the leaves break down, they provide food for the soil, which helps plants grow. The plants attract insects, some of which get eaten by the salamanders. It's a big circle of life; everything comes together to make the world go round.

Thanks to the tall trees that create a protective canopy, the forest is also shady and peaceful. This shade keeps the temperature just right for salamanders. They like it neither too hot nor too cold, and the forest gives them the perfect temperature. Remember, forests are important for all kinds of animals, not just salamanders. They are where plants, animals, and insects live together. By caring for the forest, you are helping all these amazing creatures have a happy home. So, watch out for salamanders the next time you go on a forest adventure. They have their own little paradise among the trees, and even if you don't see them, they are there.

- **Wetlands**

Water is critically important for salamanders, and they have plenty of it in wetlands. Wetlands are special places filled with lots of water, like puddles, but much bigger. Salamanders love wetlands because they need water to survive. You can find them near ponds, swamps, and marshes, where they can splash around and have fun.

10. Salamanders can also live in wetlands. Source: https://www.pexels.com/photo/gray-bird-on-ground-near-water-3124842/

In wetlands, salamanders have many different places to call home. Some like to live in shallow water, while others prefer the damp areas around the water. They hide under rocks, logs, or in the shallow holes they dig in the ground. These hiding spots keep them safe from other animals wanting to eat them.

Wetlands are full of other kinds of life. There are lots of plants and animals that live there. You can see pretty flowers like water lilies and tall plants called cattails. These plants provide a home for salamanders and give them food to eat. Salamanders can find tasty insects, worms, and even small fish to munch on among these plants.

Wetlands are important for the planet, too. They help clean the water and keep it healthy. When it rains a lot, wetlands soak up the extra water like a sponge, which helps prevent floods. Many different plants and animals rely on wetlands for their homes, so taking care of them is necessary. Unfortunately, wetlands are disappearing in some places because of certain things people do, like draining or building on top of them. When wetlands are drained, the water is removed, and the land becomes dry. This can happen because people want to use the land for farming, building houses, or making space for roads. Unfortunately, when wetlands are drained or built upon, plants and animals lose their homes. That's why you need to protect and take care of them. By doing that, you can make sure that salamanders and other wetland creatures have a safe and happy place to live.

- **Mountains**

Mountains are secret hideouts for some salamanders. They have adapted to cool temperatures and the sometimes-snowy conditions found higher up on the mountaintop. You might find them near streams, where the water is crystal clear and icy cold. These salamanders are excellent swimmers and enjoy splashing about in the mountain streams. If you look carefully, you might spot them in rocky crevices or under big rocks. These hiding places give them protection from predators and harsh weather.

11. *Mountains are secret hideouts for salamanders. Source: Grigory Heaton, CC BY-SA 4.0 <https://creativecommons.org/licenses/by-sa/4.0>, via Wikimedia Commons: https://commons.wikimedia.org/wiki/File:Inyo_mountains_salam ander_habitat.png*

Salamanders are masters of camouflage, skilled at blending in with their surroundings and making it hard for people to spot them, but if you keep your eyes peeled and are patient, you might get lucky. Some mountain-dwelling salamanders are even skilled climbers. They can be found high up in trees, among the branches and leaves. These kinds of salamanders have sticky toes that help them grip onto the tree trunks and branches.

Living in the mountains has its perks for salamanders. The cool temperatures there are just right for them. They prefer mild weather, and the mountains provide a refreshing escape from the hot summer sun. The mountains also offer different kinds of food for these salamanders. They have a taste for insects, spiders, and other small creatures. Luckily for them, the mountains are buzzing with insect life. From busy bees to crawling beetles, there's always something delicious to snack on.

Mountain habitats are not just home to salamanders. They are also home to other fascinating animals, like birds, squirrels, and even mighty bears. All these animals create a big family of different creatures. They all need each other to survive and live happily. Just like a community needs a tailor, a teacher, and a farmer, these mountain animals need each other's help and support. They work together to ensure that everyone has enough food, shelter, and a safe place to live.

- **Caves and Crevices**

Have you ever been inside a cave? It is dark, cold, and often hidden deep beneath the ground. It might feel a bit spooky to you, but for salamanders, it's perfect. Caves and crevices provide shelter and protection from the outside world. They keep salamanders safe from bright sunlight, predators, and extreme weather. You might wonder how salamanders manage to move around in the darkness. Well, they have some super senses that help them. Their skin is very sensitive to touch, allowing them to feel their way around and sense any bumps in the road. They also have excellent hearing and smell, which leads them straight to food.

12. *Caves and crevices can keep salamanders safe. Source: Greg Schechter, CC BY 2.0 <https://creativecommons.org/licenses/by/2.0>, via Wikimedia Commons: https://commons.wikimedia.org/wiki/File:Cave_Salamander_(Eurycea_lucifuga).jpg*

Caves and crevices are often damp and moist, which is perfect for salamanders. These places have the right humidity to keep their delicate skin wet and healthy. Salamanders can find plenty of insects, worms, and other small creatures to eat in these underground homes. They hunt their prey using their quick reflexes and sticky tongues.

As you've probably already guessed, it's not just salamanders that live in caves and crevices. They have many unique neighbors. Bats might hang from the ceilings, and spiders spin huge webs in the corners. It's a hidden world full of life, with each creature finding its special corner to call home.

Exploring caves can be exciting, but these places can be delicate and fragile. If you ever have the opportunity to visit a cave, make sure you are with an adult and follow any rules or guidelines to protect yourself, the environment, and the animals that live there.

- **Urban Areas**

Believe it or not, some salamanders have become quite good at living in cities. As cities grow and expand, some special salamander species have found smart ways to make their homes closer to humans. Urban areas, like parks and gardens, may appear different from forests or wetlands, but they still have lots to offer for salamanders. These smart animals have figured out how to survive and grow in these environments. They might be small, but they are very tough.

13. In cities, you can find salamanders in parks with ponds. Source: https://pixabay.com/vectors/city-village-digital-home-town-1252643/

In cities, you can find salamanders in places like parks with ponds or small streams. These areas offer water, which is important for their survival. They will likely be hiding under rocks or logs near the water's edge. Gardens and green spaces in cities also provide food for salamanders. They can find insects, worms, and other small creatures to munch on. Just like in the wild, city salamanders have a good appetite and must eat enough to stay healthy and grow.

One interesting thing about urban salamanders is that they have had to get used to living around people. Sure, salamanders might not be fond of things like buildings, large feet everywhere, and cars, which can be challenging for them, but they are very clever and have found ways to deal with these issues and find safe places to live.

Backyard ponds are little oases for salamanders in the city. If you have a pond in your backyard, you might be lucky enough to spot one. Create a safe and welcoming environment for them by setting up plants, rocks, and logs that they can hide under. Who knows, you might even get to see some cool salamander action, like swimming or catching tasty insects.

The Importance of Salamander Habitats

Salamander habitats are incredibly important. First, they provide a safe and comfortable place for salamanders to live. Just like you have your own home, salamanders need a nice place to sleep, eat, and hang with their salamander family. Different species of salamanders prefer different habitats, but all the habitats offer them everything they need to stay alive.

One important role of salamander habitats is to provide food. Salamanders are not picky eaters. They enjoy gobbling up insects, worms, small fish, and even tiny crabs. Think of their habitats as grocery stores, full of delicious treats for them to find and eat. When salamanders have plenty of food, they can grow big and strong.

Another important aspect of salamander habitats is water. Salamanders need water to survive because they breathe through their skin; if they get too dry, they cannot breathe and will die. They like to live near ponds, streams, or moist areas where they can stay hydrated. Water also helps keep their skin moist and healthy. So, without proper habitats with water, salamanders wouldn't be able to survive.

14. Be mindful of how your actions can affect Salamander's homes. Source: Hieronymus Bosch, Public domain, via Wikimedia Commons. https://commons.wikimedia.org/wiki/File:Bosch,_Hieronymus_-_The_Garden_of_Earthly_Delights,_central_panel_-_Detail_Man_riding_a_salamander_(upper_left).jpg

Salamanders are also important for their habitats. They play a role in the ecosystem, contributing to the balance of nature. For example, salamanders eat insects and other small creatures, helping control their populations. If there were too many mosquitoes buzzing around or too many beetles eating all the plants, it could throw the balance of nature out of whack, but thanks to salamanders, this doesn't happen. They help keep insect populations in check by gobbling them up. They are nature's own pest control team.

Not only do salamanders eat insects, but they also become food for other animals. They are an important part of the food chain. For example, snakes, birds, and even bigger salamanders might snack on them. This helps transfer energy from one animal to another and keeps the ecosystem running smoothly. Hold on, there's more. Salamanders are also nature's little gardeners. How, you ask? Well, some of them love to dig and burrow in the soil. As they do this, they help mix up the soil layers and create spaces for air and water to reach plant roots. This helps plants grow and provide food for the animals that eat them.

Salamander habitats also support biodiversity. Biodiversity means having many different types of plants and animals in an area. When diverse habitats are filled with different species, the entire ecosystem becomes stronger and tougher, especially when changes happen. Salamanders are a part of this diversity, and their presence adds to the richness and beauty of nature.

Sadly, some salamander habitats are being threatened by human activities such as deforestation or pollution. This is why everyone needs to learn more about these things to protect and preserve these places. You can do your part by spreading the word at school, planting native plants, and being mindful of how your actions can affect their homes. By understanding and appreciating the importance of these habitats, everyone can work together so salamanders and other animals have a safe and happy place to call home.

Chapter Three: Salamander Features and Behaviors

Are you ready for the nitty-gritty details about what makes salamanders one of the coolest animals around? Get ready to learn about all their body parts and the amazing things they can do. In this chapter, you will take a closer look at the remarkable adaptations that make salamanders so special. You'll be so impressed by the secrets behind their slimy yet oh-so-important skin and the science behind their regenerative skills. From their lightning-speed swimming skills to their clever ways of catching their dinner, salamanders have some seriously amazing moves. However, before you get into it, there are a few important words you need to understand:

1. **Amphibians:** Salamanders are a type of amphibian. Amphibians are animals that can live both on land and in water. They have special body parts that allow them to survive in both environments.

2. **Regeneration**: Salamanders have an incredible ability called regeneration. This means that if a

salamander loses a body part, such as a tail or a toe, it can grow back.

3. **Nocturnal:** Salamanders are often active during the night. They are nocturnal creatures, which means they prefer to come out and do their business when it's dark outside. Their eyes are specially made to see in low-light conditions, allowing them to find their way and hunt for food at night.

4. **Ectothermic:** Salamanders are ectothermic animals. This means that their body temperature changes with the temperature of their surroundings. So, if it's cold outside, their body temperature will be colder; if it's warm, their body temperature will be warmer. They rely on the environment to regulate their body temperature.

Now that you've got your vocabulary sorted, you're ready for the real deal.

Salamander Anatomy

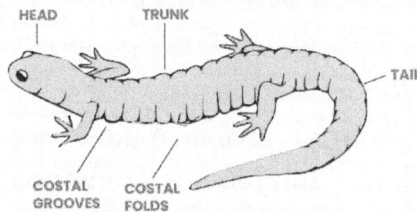

15. Salamander Anatomy. Source:
https://www.researchgate.net/publication/356174861/figure/fig22
/AS:1089412188373033@1636747514606/Salamander-external-anatomy.png

- **Body Shape**

Salamanders have long, slim bodies that are incredibly useful for their amphibian lifestyle. Their bodies are like flexible tubes that allow them to squeeze into small spaces and explore hidden nooks and crannies. When searching for food or looking for a place to hide, salamanders can wiggle through narrow spaces, under rocks, or between plants, reaching places that other animals might find difficult to get to.

Their long and slender bodies help them swim smoothly in the water and with great speed. They are shaped like rockets or torpedoes, and this streamlined shape reduces water resistance, allowing them to glide effortlessly through the water. Whether they are chasing after prey or just swimming around their watery homes, salamanders are well-adapted to life in aquatic environments.

But they don't just stick to the water—they are also masters on land. Their bodies are perfect for moving on different kinds of land. Their long and slender shape reduces drag, making it easier for them to walk or crawl. Whether climbing rocks, crawling through bushes, or walking on the forest floor, their bodies allow them to move easily and quickly.

- **Skin**

Firstly, salamander skin is smooth and wet. It feels a bit slimy because it has special glands that make a slimy layer of mucus. This slimy layer helps keep the skin wet and slippery. See it like a raincoat that keeps the wetness in and dryness out. But the sliminess isn't just for show. Salamanders use their mucus to protect themselves. It can taste unpleasant to some animals that might want to eat them, so technically, it is also a defense mechanism.

Another cool thing about salamander skin is that it can breathe. This is called "cutaneous respiration." When they're in the water or moist environments, oxygen from the water or air passes through their skin and into their bodies. This breathable skin is also very sensitive, so they can also feel things through their skin, like vibrations in the water or on land. It helps them detect movement and find their prey or hide from predators. And here's another interesting fact: salamanders can change the color of their skin. Some kinds of salamanders can blend in with their surroundings by changing their skin color. It helps them hide from predators or sneak up on their prey.

Salamanders are also ectothermic. They can't make their bodies warm like humans or other mammals can. Instead, they lay down in the sun or find cooler spots to stay comfortable. Their skin helps with this. When they want to warm up, they absorb heat through their skin from the sun or warm areas; to cool down, they find a shady spot or wet area to lower their body temperature.

- **Limbs and Tail**

Salamanders have four legs, like a cat, but their legs are designed for different things. They help them walk on land and swim in the water. Each leg has little toes, just like your fingers and toes, but salamander toes are often a bit longer and, honestly, a bit cooler. These special toes help them grip and stick to things. They can use them to climb rocks, hold onto branches, or dig into the ground.

Now, the tail. Salamanders have a long and very strong tail. It helps them swim easily and change direction quickly in the water. But it isn't only for swimming. Salamanders use their tail on land to keep their balance as they move around. It helps them stay steady and prevents them from tipping over. Some salamanders can even drop their tail if they are being attacked. It's a trick they use to distract predators. The lost tail will wiggle around, making the predator think it caught the salamander while the little hero escapes to safety. Don't worry, though, the salamander will grow a new tail later.

- **Eyes**

Salamander eyes are usually big, round, and rarely miss a thing. They have a unique shape that helps them see things from different angles. Their eyes are on the sides of their head, meaning they can see in almost all directions. This helps them spot danger or find tasty insects to eat.

Here's a neat fact: Some salamanders have better vision underwater than on land. Their eyes are smaller but adapted to see clearly in the water. They can spot movement in the water and find their prey easily, but that's not all. These salamanders also have an extra eyelid called a "nictitating membrane." It's a see-through curtain that covers their eyes and protects them from dirt, water, and bright sunlight—an important body part if you're going to live in water. Finally, salamanders also have good nighttime vision. They can see well in the dark, handy for nocturnal animals.

- **Teeth and Tongue**

Regarding teeth, salamanders have a unique situation. You see, their teeth are tiny and sharp, but they're not like your teeth as they can't use them to chew or tear food apart. Plus, they have an extra set of teeth, which is actually located on the roof of their mouths. Their tiny teeth are very useful, though, because they help them grab onto their food. When they catch insects or other small creatures, they use their teeth to hold onto them tightly while swallowing them whole.

Here's a really fun part: salamanders have a special trick with their tongues. They can shoot their tongues out really fast to catch their prey. It's a lightning-fast tongue attack. When they spot a delicious insect, they quickly flick their tongue out and snatch it up. This movement is so fast that you may miss it if you blink. Their tongues are stretchy like rubber bands, allowing them to reach out and grab their food. Not all salamanders have tongues that shoot out, though. Some have sticky tongues instead. All they have to do is touch their prey with their tongue, and it sticks to it like glue.

- **External Gills**

When baby salamanders hatch from their eggs, little feathery gills stick out from the sides of their heads. These gills are delicate, leafy structures that help them take in oxygen from the water. These gills have tiny blood vessels that help absorb oxygen, and as water flows over them, oxygen passes into the blood, and carbon dioxide, which is what they breathe out, goes back into the water. However, as baby salamanders grow up, they go through a change called metamorphosis, the same way a caterpillar changes into a butterfly. During this change, their gills start to disappear, and some develop lungs, just like you have. Once they become adults, they no longer have external gills. Instead, they breathe air through their lungs or the skin.

Salamander Regeneration

When a salamander loses a tail or a limb, something incredible happens. Instead of staying injured or handicapped forever, their body has the incredible power to grow it back. Here's how it works: When a salamander gets hurt and loses a body part, special cells in their body called "regenerative cells" get to work. These regenerative cells are little workers that start rebuilding the lost body parts.

First, the regenerative cells start making a special tissue called a "blastema." This blastema is a blueprint for the new body part. It tells the cells what to do and how to grow it back. Then, these amazing regenerative cells start multiplying and turning into different types of cells: muscle cells, bone cells, and skin cells. All these cells work together to rebuild the lost body part, following the instructions of the blastema.

Slowly but surely, the new body part starts to grow back, and over time, the salamander's tail or limb regains its shape and function, becoming just like it was before. What's even more mind-blowing is that the regenerated body part is almost identical to the original one in structure and function. It's literally a perfect copy. This regenerative power is something that makes salamanders very special. While most animals, including humans, are unable to regrow body parts, salamanders pretty much heal themselves and grow back what they have lost. Scientists are still trying to understand the secrets behind salamander regeneration, hoping to learn from them and apply this knowledge to help people who have lost body parts, like soldiers or people who have had accidents.

You know, sometimes, for different reasons, some body parts start to break down or not work as well as they used to. This is called degeneration. But if scientists can figure out regeneration, it could slow down or even reverse the degeneration process. It could make people feel better and not have so many aches and pains. They will be able to regrow their body parts, just like salamanders can.

Do Salamanders Communicate with Each Other?

Yes, salamanders do communicate with each other, but they don't use words like humans do. Instead, they have their own unique ways of talking to each other. One way salamanders communicate is by using unusual scents or smells. They release scents that other salamanders can smell. It sends a message through the air. These scents help salamanders find each other and tell them things like, "Hey, I'm here" or "This is my spot, stay away."

16. Salamanders do communicate with each other. Source: English: NPS Photo, Public domain, via Wikimedia Commons. https://commons.wikimedia.org/wiki/File:Two_marbled_salamanders_(Ambystoma_opacum)_(8643f852-f6b4-41d1-8efe-2711e4097b0d).jpg

Salamanders also use body language to talk to each other. They might wiggle their bodies, puff up their throats, or even do weird dances. They use their bodies to say, "Hello," "I'm feeling happy," or "I want to be your friend." Sometimes, male salamanders make special sounds to get the attention of the females. They might make chirping or clicking sounds. It's like singing a song to say, "Hey, look at me. I like you. Do you like me?" All these ways of communication help salamanders find friends, show off their qualities, or warn others to stay away.

Chapter Four: Life Cycle of Salamanders

A life cycle is the process that every living thing goes through. It's a journey that starts when something is born or hatched and ends when it grows old or dies. First, there is the beginning stage. This is when a new living thing is born or hatched from an egg. It starts small and has a lot of growing to do. Then comes the growth stage. During this time, the living thing gets bigger and stronger. It learns new things and develops new abilities. Just like when you grow taller and learn more things as you age.

Next, there is the maturity stage. This is when the living thing is fully grown and can do everything it's meant to do. After maturity, there is the reproduction stage, where all living things have babies or lay eggs to continue the life cycle. This is how new generations are created. Finally, there is the aging stage. As time passes, the living thing gets older and might not be as strong or active as before. Eventually, it reaches the end of its life cycle and passes away. The life cycle is a natural process that happens to all living things. It's a way for new life to come into the world and for the cycle to continue.

17. *Salamander's life cycle. Source: Internet Archive Book Images, No restrictions, via Wikimedia Commons. https://commons.wikimedia.org/wiki/File:Amours_des_salamand res_aquatiques_- _et_developpement_du_tetard_de_ces_salamandres_depuis_l%2 70euf_jusqu%27a_l%27animal_parfait_(1821)_(18165947581).jpg*

The Fascinating Transformation from Eggs to Adults

Salamanders have an incredible life cycle involving some truly interesting changes. It all starts with the eggs. Female salamanders lay their eggs in particular places, like ponds or streams. The eggs are usually attached to underwater plants or rocks to keep them safe. Now, these eggs might not look like much at first. They are small and jelly-like, almost like clear bubbles. But inside each egg, a tiny baby salamander is waiting to meet the world.

18. Salamander egg. Source: The Cosmonaut, CC BY-SA 2.5 CA
<https://creativecommons.org/licenses/by-sa/2.5/ca/deed.en>,
via Wikimedia Commons.
https://commons.wikimedia.org/wiki/File:Salamander_eggmass.j
pg

As time passes, something wonderful happens. The eggs start to develop, and the baby salamanders are growing within them. They have all the parts they need to become salamanders, but they're not quite ready to come out into the world just yet. After a while, the eggs hatch, and the baby salamanders enter the water. At this stage, they are called larvae and look quite different from adult salamanders. They have long tails, gills for breathing underwater, and no legs. They almost resemble tiny fish or tadpoles.

Now, the larvae have an important job to do. They swim around and eat small animals, like insects and tiny plants, to grow bigger and stronger. They have a big appetite because they need enough energy for an amazing change coming up soon. This change is a process called metamorphosis. During metamorphosis, the larvae begin to change their looks and develop into adult salamanders.

First, they start growing legs. Two little front legs emerge, followed by two back legs. They learn to walk for the very first time. Their tails also become shorter and less obvious at first. At the same time, their gills start to disappear, and something new takes their place: lungs or that special slimy skin. This means that the salamanders are getting ready to leave their watery homes and explore the land. They are becoming true amphibians, capable of living in water and land.

Once the change is complete, the young salamanders are called juveniles. They look like small versions of adult salamanders but with brighter colors and patterns. They head out onto the land, walking about in the forests, meadows, or wherever their habitat may be. They continue to grow and develop, becoming stronger and more independent with each passing day.

As the juveniles grow older, they reach adulthood. Adult salamanders have fully developed bodies, including lungs or slimy skin for breathing air and all four legs. They are skilled hunters, using their long tongues to catch insects, worms, and other small animals. Some adult salamanders even have special adaptations, like sticky tongues or bright colors, to attract mates or defend themselves. Adult salamanders find a mate during the breeding season and lay eggs, starting the whole life cycle over again. And so, the amazing journey of transformation from eggs to adults continues, generation after generation.

Salamander Mating Ritual

When it's time for salamander breeding, the male salamanders become very active. They begin their search for a special someone, a female salamander, to be their mate. They use their keen senses, like their sense of smell and sharp eyes, to find her, and once they do, they want to impress her. The male salamander may perform a courtship dance to catch her attention. He might wiggle his body, wave his tail, or even make funny movements. It's a dance-off just for salamanders.

The male's dance is not only about showing off his moves but also about leaving behind a nice scent that tells the female he's ready to breed. It's a salamander love note with a special perfume. If the female is interested, she joins in the dance. They swim or walk together, showing off their dance moves. They might touch each other gently or rub their bodies together. It's their way of saying, "You're amazing, and I want to be with you."

During this dance, the male salamander gives his sperm to the female. He has a special body part called a cloaca, which allows him to pass the sperm to the female salamander. It's a special delivery system for baby-making cells. Once the female has received the sperm, she stores it inside her body. She doesn't have the babies right away, though. She patiently waits for the right time to lay her eggs. She finds the best place to lay her eggs when the time is right. She prefers areas like freshwater ponds, streams, or even damp soil. You see, the eggs need to be in a wet environment for them to grow properly. The female carefully attaches her eggs to underwater plants, rocks, or other surfaces. She might lay them in clusters or a long, string-like shape. She takes her time to create a cozy nursery for her future babies.

Once the eggs are laid, her job is done. She leaves the eggs behind and goes on her way. The eggs need to be in water to survive and grow because it gives them the right temperature and oxygen, they need to develop into baby salamanders.

How Long Do Salamanders Live?

Different species of salamanders have different lifespans. For example, the axolotl, a type of salamander that lives in Mexico, is the only salamander that stays in its larval form throughout its entire life. It doesn't go through metamorphosis like other salamanders. In the wild, axolotls have a lifespan of around 10 to 15 years, but some axolotls living as pets or in conservatories with proper care and habitat conditions can live even longer.

19. The axolotl, a type of salamander, can live up to 15 years. Source: Amandasofiarana, CC BY-SA 4.0 <https://creativecommons.org/licenses/by-sa/4.0>, via Wikimedia Commons: https://commons.wikimedia.org/wiki/File:Axolotl_ambystoma_m exicanum_anfibio_ASAG.jpg

Another fascinating salamander species is the Japanese giant salamander. These amazing amphibians are one of the largest salamanders in the world, growing up to five feet long. They also have an incredibly long lifespan. Japanese giant salamanders can live for more than 65 years in the wild. That's longer than many other animals of the same size. They are known for their long lives and have become a symbol of longevity and good luck in Japanese culture.

Moving on to another species, the tiger salamander is a common salamander found in North America. They have a regular salamander life cycle, starting as larvae in the water, like little fish with gills. As they grow, they undergo metamorphosis and develop lungs to breathe air, just like humans. These salamanders can live for around 10 to 16 years in the wild.

Next, you have the red-spotted newt, another interesting salamander species. They start as water larvae, then transform into a land-dwelling juvenile stage called an "eft." At this stage, the eft has bright orange or red coloring, which protects them from animals that might want to eat them. After a few years, they transform again into water-dwelling adults who go on to live for about 12 to 15 years.

Last but not least, there is the fire salamander. Fire salamanders are known for their striking black and yellow patterns. They are found in parts of Europe and have a lifespan of around 14 to 30 years. These particular salamanders have a slower reproductive cycle compared to some other species, and scientists think it may be the reason for their longer lifespan.

Factors That Affect Salamander Lifespan

There are a few things that can determine how long salamanders live:

1. **Type of Salamander**: Different types of salamanders have different lifespans. Some live longer than others. For example, the Japanese giant salamander can live for more than 50 years, while smaller salamanders might not live that long.

2. **Home and Environment**: The place where salamanders live is important. They need a clean, safe home with enough food, water, and places to hide. If their home gets polluted or damaged, it can make them ill, and they will not live as long.

3. **Other Animals**: Some animals, like birds, snakes, and fish, enjoy eating salamanders. If salamanders can avoid being caught by these animals, they have a better chance of living longer. Being good at hiding or moving quickly helps them stay safe.

4. **Staying Healthy**: Like people, salamanders need to stay healthy to live longer. They need to eat good food, have clean water to drink, and live in a suitable place. Sometimes, they can get ill from diseases or bugs that weaken them and then not live for long.

5. **Breeding:** Having babies can affect how long salamanders live. Some salamanders have a lot of babies, and it takes a lot of their energy. This might affect how long they live. Other salamanders have fewer babies and can use more of their energy to live longer.

6. **Genes:** Genes are the instructions that determine how living things grow and behave. Salamanders have genes that can make them live longer or shorter lives. It's the same way some people inherit traits from their parents, like eye color or hair type.

Chapter Five: Salamanders in the Ecosystem

A world without salamanders might be a little weirder than you think. Salamanders have a critically important job in the environment and with other animals. They help keep pesky bugs under control and even help plants grow, and that's just two jobs. They have more. Salamanders help the world without people even realizing it. They work quietly in the background to make sure everything stays balanced and healthy. In this chapter, you'll be learning all about the many jobs salamanders have in the environment so you can be thankful for all the ways they make the world a better place.

20. Salamanders keep pesky bugs under control. Source: Pacific Southwest Region USFWS from Sacramento, US, Public domain, via Wikimedia Commons.
https://commons.wikimedia.org/wiki/File:Food_chain_in_action!
_(28015672023).png

The Role of Salamanders in the Food Chain

At the very beginning of the food chain, some plants and algae make their own food using sunlight. They do this thing called 'photosynthesis.' Then, tiny bugs like beetles and caterpillars eat these plants and algae, and the salamanders get involved. Here's how:

- **Insect Control**: Salamanders are awesome at catching insects. They are excellent insect hunters and have an important job keeping the bug population balanced. Salamanders have really big appetites when it comes to insects and spiders. They love to munch on annoying bugs like mosquitoes, flies, and ants. By eating these pests, they ensure there aren't too many of them buzzing around and bothering people. They are natural pest control experts who gobble up the bugs and help keep the surroundings more comfortable.

- **Amphibian Snacks**: Salamanders are not only great insect hunters but also become tasty snacks for other animals higher up in the food chain. Some animals really enjoy the taste of salamanders. Snakes, birds, fish, and other bigger amphibians like frogs and turtles think salamanders are quite delicious, so when these predators eat salamanders, it helps them stay healthy and strong. Salamanders are an important source of food for these hungry animals, helping them grow and survive in their habitats. It's a natural buffet where the salamanders keep the food chain balanced and everyone well-fed.

- **Natural Recycling**: Did you know some salamanders, like the red-backed salamanders, have a special diet? They eat things like fallen leaves, twigs, and other stuff on the forest floor, and here's the best part: when they eat this stuff, they help break it down into smaller pieces, like living recycling machines. Breaking down these things helps the pieces turn into soil more quickly. This process is called decomposition. When that happens, important nutrients are released back into the soil, becoming food for plants. So, salamanders actually help plants grow and keep the whole forest ecosystem healthy. Their job is to keep the forest floor clean and make sure that everything gets recycled and used again.

- **Predator Avoidance:** Salamanders are clever when it comes to staying safe from other animals that might want to eat them. They have a couple of tricks to avoid becoming someone's dinner. Some salamanders have bright, flashy colors or patterns that act like warning signs. These colors tell predators, 'Stay away! I might be toxic or yucky to eat.' But that's not all. Some salamanders have another power. They can release a sticky or smelly goo from their skin when afraid. This sticky or stinky stuff makes them really unappetizing to any animal that tries to eat them. It's their way of saying, 'You won't like the taste of me.' These special defenses keep salamanders safe and ensure they remain in the food chain because if they are all eaten too quickly, they won't get a chance to do all the other important jobs they have to do.

Salamanders as an Indicator Species

Salamanders help scientists understand if an ecosystem is healthy or not. Salamanders are very sensitive and feel even the smallest changes in their environment. When something is wrong, salamander populations may start to go down. This is a sign that something isn't quite right in their home.

Picture a beautiful forest with lots of trees, plants, and animals. In this forest, there are many different kinds of salamanders. They live in the cozy shade of the trees and near streams or ponds. Salamanders need clean water and a safe place to hide, like under logs or rocks. They have that special moist skin that helps them breathe, so they like to stay in damp areas.

But sometimes, people might do things that harm the environment. For example, if harmful chemicals or pollution get into the water, it can make it unsafe for salamanders to live there. Pollution is a poison that hurts their sensitive bodies. It's like trying to breathe in smelly air or drink dirty water. Salamanders can't survive in such conditions, so their numbers may start to decrease. Some of them go to find another place to live, while others get ill and die.

21. Water pollution causes the water to be unsafe for salamanders. Source: https://pixabay.com/vectors/dead-ecology-effluent-fish-lake-158707/

Habitat destruction is another problem. Salamanders lose their homes when people cut down too many trees or remove logs and rocks. Imagine if someone took away your bedroom or your favorite hiding spot. Without these special places, salamanders can't find food or escape from predators. Their population might get smaller and smaller as a result.

Scientists care a lot about salamanders and the ecosystems in which they live. They study them to learn more about the health of the environment. They go out into the forest and look for salamanders. By counting how many salamanders they find, they can get an idea of how many are living in that area. If they find fewer salamanders than before, it could mean there's something wrong. When scientists notice a decline in salamander numbers, they investigate to find out why. They might test the water to see if it's polluted or check if there are enough logs and rocks for the salamanders to hide under. By understanding the reasons behind the decline, they can work on finding solutions to help the salamanders and restore balance to the ecosystem.

Scientists work to ensure that forests and all the creatures that live there stay healthy. They also want to protect the salamanders' homes and make sure they are doing okay. By studying salamanders, scientists can learn a lot about what's happening in the environment and take action to make things better. So, the presence or absence of salamanders in an area tells scientists a story. It helps them understand if the ecosystem is doing well or if there are problems that need to be fixed. Think of salamanders as ambassadors, speaking on behalf of the forest and the other animals. They are a reminder to take care of the environment so that they and all the other creatures can continue to live happily ever after.

Salamanders as Habitat Engineers

Did you know that some salamanders are fantastic diggers? One type of salamander, the mole salamander, is especially good at digging. They have strong front legs and sharp claws that help them burrow into the ground or through piles of leaves. When these salamanders start digging, they create tunnels and burrows underground—some secret hideout. These tiny spaces they create become cozy homes for other animals. Picture a big apartment building, but underground.

Who lives in these underground homes? Well, all sorts of animals. Insects like beetles, ants, and spiders might move in. They find safety and shelter in these tiny spaces. Earthworms, wriggly garden helpers, also like to live in the tunnels made by salamanders. Sometimes, even smaller salamanders make their homes in these burrows, too. These underground hideaways are important for all these animals. They protect them from predators like birds or other animals that might want to eat them. The burrows also protect them from bad weather, like heavy rain or hot sun. It's comfortable, hidden, and really tiny.

22. *Salamanders find the perfect place to live by digging. Source: U.S. Geological Survey from Reston, VA, USA, CC0, via Wikimedia Commons:* *https://commons.wikimedia.org/wiki/File:Shenandoah_Salamand er_and_Climate_(10741154185).jpg*

But why do salamanders dig these burrows in the first place? Well, salamanders need a cool and moist place to live, as you know. They find the perfect spot to stay comfortably damp by digging into the soil or leaf litter. When salamanders dig and create these burrows, they also help the environment. How? Their digging mixes up the soil and the leaves. This helps make the soil healthier and full of nutrients. These tiny gardeners help plants grow and provide food for other animals, some of which they might eat for energy so that they can continue their work, that is, if they don't get eaten themselves. It's called a food chain for a reason.

Now you know salamanders are literal heroes with special abilities and important jobs. You've learned they are habitat engineers, creating comfy homes for other animals with their burrowing and digging skills. They help mix up the soil and leaves, making the environment healthier for plants and providing food for other animals. They're also an environmental clean-up crew, eating insects and keeping the ecosystem in balance.

Salamanders teach you that everyone, no matter who you are, is important in the big picture of nature. They show that everyone is connected and that by taking care of the environment and appreciating your uniqueness and the uniqueness of different animals, you can help create a happy and successful ecosystem. So, celebrate salamanders and all the amazing things they do. Whether digging tunnels or eating those nasty bugs, they are true champions of the natural world. By protecting their habitats and learning from their example, you can make a positive difference in your own communities and help preserve the beauty and balance of ecosystems for future generations.

Chapter Six: Fun Salamander Facts and Activities

You have made it to the final chapter, and now it's time for some exciting and interesting facts about salamanders. Not only will you become smarter, but you will also have exciting stories to share with your friends and family. You'll definitely be the star of the next science class discussion or nature walk adventure. You are ready to become a salamander expert.

23. Salamanders are ancient! Source: Internet Archive Book Images, No restrictions, via Wikimedia Commons. https://commons.wikimedia.org/wiki/File:Image_from_page_59 _of_%22Water_reptiles_of_the_past_and_present%22_(1914)_(1 4586507527).jpg

Fun Salamander Facts

1. **Salamanders Are Ancient:** Once upon a time, long before the dinosaurs, there were salamanders. One particular kind of salamander, called Triassurus sixtelae, lived a very, very long time ago, around 230 million years ago, during a period called the Triassic. In 2020, scientists discovered a fossil of one of these ancient salamanders in a place called Kyrgyzstan. It turned out to be the oldest salamander ever found. These old salamander bones give scientists clues about how salamanders first started to exist and how they differ from other amphibians, like frogs. Before this discovery, the oldest salamander fossils were from a later time, called the Jurassic, and were found in China.

2. **Axolotl Can Repair Its Spinal Cord:** The axolotl is one of the few animals in the world able to regrow their spinal cord. In humans and many other animals, spinal cord injuries are often permanent and can lead to paralysis. However, if axolotls hurt their spinal cord and can't move, they have the power to fix it and move again. Scientists are amazed by this and are trying to learn from the axolotls to help people whose spinal cords are hurt or not working properly. They hope that by studying axolotls, they can find new ways to help those who can't move because of spinal cord injuries.

3. **Salamanders Can Taste with Their Skin**: Not only can salamanders breathe through their skin, but they can also "taste" things with it. They have special cells on their skin called chemoreceptors

that help them detect different chemicals. Think tiny taste buds, but all over their body. These chemoreceptors help salamanders find food to eat, friends to hang out with, and even figure out where they are going. So, while you use your nose and tongue to taste things, salamanders can use their skin to understand what's happening around them.

4. **Too Many Salamanders in North America:** Did you know North America is home to many different salamanders? It has more salamander species than any other place in the world. And guess what? Scientists think there are even more species that are yet to be discovered. Most of these salamanders live in the Appalachian Mountains. It's a hot spot for them. There's something sad, though. These salamanders are in danger. There's a disease called salamander chytrid disease that is hurting them. They're getting very ill, and it's not good for their population. One of the reasons this disease spreads is because people bring salamanders from other places to keep as pets. Some pet salamanders, like fire belly newts, can carry bacteria that make other salamanders ill and possibly die off.

5. **Hellbenders Are the Only Cryptobranchidae Family Found in North America:** There is a type of salamander in North America called the Hellbender. It's unique because it belongs to the same family as the giant salamanders from China and Japan. This salamander lives in the Appalachian Mountain range and is a bit bigger than other salamanders in the area, growing up to 27 inches long. Although, on average, they are

about 17 inches long. They have wrinkled skin and fewer toes, and they do not have gills like other salamanders. If you ever see a hellbender in the wild, do not catch it or try to keep it as a pet. Instead, take a picture if you can, let it go back to its home, and then tell the people in charge of taking care of animals in your state so they can keep track of them. Everyone must do their part to protect these special salamanders and let them live happily in their natural habitats.

6. **Hellbenders Cannot Regenerate:** Hellbenders don't have the special power to regain their lost limbs. They are not like other salamanders in this way.

7. **Salamanders Have No Vocal Cords**: Did you know that salamanders can't make sounds like other animals? They don't have vocal cords like humans or other animals. Instead, they make different kinds of noises when they want to communicate. They might squeak, click, snap, or even make kissing-like sounds by moving their jaws or blowing out air. Some scientists think that salamanders might also use high-frequency noises to talk to each other, but they can't say for sure because salamanders don't have the right ears to pick up those sounds.

8. **Salamanders Are Venom-Proof:** Salamanders are so cool that they are immune to venom. Most animals can't do this—you can't do this—so it's unique. They have super proteins in their blood that act like a shield against venom. These proteins grab onto the venom and stop it from doing any damage.

Even though salamanders can resist venom, they still have to be careful. They have enemies like venomous snakes and spiders that could hurt them. So, even though they can handle the venom, they prefer to avoid these dangerous animals. They are smart and know it's better to stay away from trouble than to get into a fight.

Activities and Projects for Kids

- **Salamander Dress Up**

Why spend all day looking at salamanders when you can look LIKE one? It's time to dress up. Find colorful costumes or make your own salamander outfit. Cut out a salamander face shape from strong paper or cardboard. Decorate it with bright colors, patterns, and maybe some glitter. Attach strings or elastic bands to the sides to wear it like a mask. Get creative and make a long, wiggly tail out of fabric or paper strips. Use safety pins or tape to attach it to the back of your pants or skirt. You can also make frills using colorful paper or fabric strips and attach them to your mask or wear them around your wrists. Pick out green, brown, or other brightly colored clothes that can pass for a salamander's skin. Wear them to complete your salamander look.

Once you're all dressed up, pretend to be your favorite salamander species and make up stories about your adventures in the wild, exploring forests and lakes just like real salamanders do. You can also gather your friends and have a pretend salamander party. Each of you can take turns showing off your cool salamander costumes and sharing interesting facts about the salamander you're dressed as. You can even come up with special salamander dances or secret salamander greetings.

- **Salamander Obstacle Course**

Do you have what it takes to move like a salamander? How about creating a mini-obstacle course and testing your crawling and maneuvering skills? First, arrange some pillows or cushions in a line to create a soft pathway. Pretend they are the rocks and logs salamanders crawl over in their natural habitat. Then, get some tunnels or create your own using blankets or cardboard boxes. These will represent the tight spaces salamanders love to wiggle through or hide in.

Now, it's time to put your skills to the test. Start at one end of the obstacle course and crawl like a salamander, using your hands and knees to move smoothly over the pillows. Imagine you're crossing a rocky stream or a bumpy forest floor, just like salamanders do. As you reach the tunnels, wiggle your way through, pretending you're squeezing into a cozy hiding spot or exploring a secret underground tunnel. Take your time; there's no rush... unless a bird is trying to EAT YOU, and then you need to hide quickly.

To make it even more exciting, you can time yourself and try to beat your own record on each run. Get your friends or family members to join in and see who can complete the course the fastest or with the most style. Safety first, though. Make sure the obstacles are stable and secure, and get an adult to supervise, just in case.

- **Salamander Movie Night**

Pick a movie or show that's all about salamanders. Look for ones that show where they live, how they move, and all the awesome stuff they can do. You can find animated movies or nature shows that make learning about salamanders easy and fun. As you watch, pay close attention to the different kinds of salamanders and what makes them special. See how they crawl, swim, and even regenerate their tails.

After the movie, you can draw pictures or write down the cool facts you learned. Maybe even make a little "salamander movie review" to share with your friends and family. It's a fun way to remember what you discovered and get others excited about salamanders, too.

- **Salamander Outdoor Adventure**

Grab your explorer gear because it's about time you head out into nature to search for some salamanders. As you walk, keep your eyes peeled for small bodies of water like ponds, streams, or wet areas. Salamanders love hanging out near these places. Look carefully under rocks, logs, or leaves because you might find one hiding there. Remember to be gentle and respectful if you find a salamander or its home. Salamanders are delicate animals, so make sure you don't disturb them. Instead, observe them from a safe distance, using your eyes and ears only.

You might see salamanders with different colors and patterns. Some might be green, while others could be brown, yellow, or red. Pause and just enjoy the beauty of nature around you. Listen to the sounds of birds chirping and feel the breeze on your face. If you're lucky, you might even spot other cool animals like frogs, turtles, or birds sharing the salamanders' home. Remember that you are a guest there, so you must leave everything as you found it. You don't want to harm any plants or animals during your adventure.

Conclusion

You have completed your adventure through the exciting world of salamanders. You've become an explorer of nature with more knowledge today than you had yesterday. You finally understand the incredible habitats where salamanders live and why they are so important. Salamanders have found their special homes in nature, from lush forests to peaceful wetlands. By learning about where they live and how they behave, you can see how they have survived for millions of years.

Salamanders are a reminder that nature is full of surprises and that even when things are tough, there's always room for growth and change. They teach the power of adaptation and toughness. These tiny creatures have changed and adapted over a long time to live in different places. They have made homes in various environments, from dark caves to tall mountains. They are living proof that it is possible to stay safe and use the things around you to survive. So, when you've finished reading this book, remember to keep learning, exploring, and respecting wildlife. When you see animals in their homes, give them space and treat them kindly. Share what you've learned with others to inspire them to appreciate and protect the incredible creatures that share our planet. You are now a nature champion and a friend to salamanders, and you have a job to do. By sharing your knowledge, you can teach others to respect and protect all the animals that make the world so special. So, stay curious and keep making a difference. Let the spirit of adventure guide you as you continue to uncover the secrets of nature and celebrate all the creatures that make it so cool.

Don't forget to leave a review and share your thoughts. Did you enjoy the book? What were your favorite parts? Did you learn something new? Are you excited to meet a salamander? Your feedback is valuable, so leave a comment and spread the word.

References

Books, B. I. B. (2016, June 8). Snakes, Salamanders, Newts, and More! Cool Reptiles and Amphibians for Kids - Children's Biological Science of Reptiles & Amphibians Books. Baby IQ Builder Books.

Francis, E. T. B. (1934, January 1). The Anatomy of the Salamander.

Griffiths, R. (1996, January 1). Newts and Salamanders of Europe. T. & A. D. Poyser.

H., & Weinfurter, M. (2019, August 5). Salamander 101. HowExpert.

McIntyre, G. (2017, September 27). The Newt Fact and Picture Book. Createspace Independent Publishing Platform.

Sparreboom, M. (2014, September 8). Salamanders of the Old World. BRILL.

Squire, A. O. (2007, January 1). Chinese Giant Salamander. Bearport Publishing.

Strattin, L. (2019, September 14). Facts about the Salamander.

Turner, T. (2017, March 13). The Axolotl Do Your Kids Know This? Createspace Independent Publishing Platform.

Weber, F. (2021, December 30). Fun Facts about Axolotl

Made in United States
Orlando, FL
21 May 2025